PIONEER DAYS
Moments in History
by Shirley Jordan

Perfection Learning® CA

About the Author

Shirley Jordan is a retired elementary school teacher and principal. Currently a lecturer in the teacher-training program at California State University, Fullerton, California, she sees exciting things happening in the world of social studies. Shirley loves to travel—with a preference for sites important to U.S. history.

She has had more than 50 travel articles published in recent years. It was through her travels that she became interested in "moments in history," those ironic and little-known stories that make one exclaim, "I didn't know that!" Such stories are woven throughout her books.

Cover Photo: Denver Public Library
Designer: Deborah Lea Bell

Image Credits: Art Today pp. 8, 12, 17, 30, 32, 34, 37, 38, 41, 47, 56, 57, 58, 59, 62; Denver Public Library pp. 4, 35, 40, 50, 51; Kansas State Historical Society p. 23; Library of Congress pp. 1, 3, 5, 6, 9, 13, 15, 18, 20, 21, 22, 23, 24, 25, 27, 48, 49, 52, 53; Missouri Historical Society p. 19; St Louis Post Dispatch p. 61

For information, contact
Perfection Learning® Corporation
1000 North Second Avenue,
P.O. Box 500, Logan, Iowa 51546-0500.
Tel: 1-800-831-4190 • Fax: 1-800-543-2745
perfectionlearning.com
Paperback ISBN 0-7891-2912-4
Cover Craft® ISBN 0-7807-8160-0

Table of Contents

A Timeline of Important Events

1803	President Thomas Jefferson signs the Louisiana Purchase.
1804–1806	Lewis and Clark journey from St. Louis to the Pacific Ocean and back.
1805–1806	Zebulon Pike finds the spot where the Mississippi River begins.
1806–1807	On his second trip, Pike explores the southern and western parts of the Louisiana Purchase. He enters territory owned by Spain. He is arrested and guided home.
1807	Manuel Lisa begins fur trading in the land discovered by Lewis and Clark.
1807–1808	John Colter explores the Rocky Mountains. He is the first white man to see Yellowstone Park.
1810–1811	John Jacob Astor forms the Pacific Fur Company. He sends out two groups to explore the West.
1811	An earthquake strikes the frontier town of New Madrid, Missouri.
1812	War begins between the U.S. and England.
1819–1820	Stephen H. Long leads a group into the Rocky Mountains. He reports that the land is not of much use. He climbs Pike's Peak.
1822	Mexico gains independence from Spain.
1825	Jim Bridger finds the Great Salt Lake.

1826	Jedediah Smith takes a southern path to California.
1833	Joe Walker and his party find the Yosemite Valley.
1841	The first covered wagons set out on the Oregon Trail.
1842	John Charles Fremont and Kit Carson explore the Rocky Mountains and the Oregon Territory.
1846	The United States and Britain sign the Oregon Treaty. The 49th parallel is named the line between the U.S. and Canada in the Northwest.
1846–1847	The Mormons travel to the Great Salt Lake. They begin building a new city.
1847	Mexico gives up the Texas and New Mexico territories to the U.S.
1848	Gold is discovered in California.
1853	The U.S. signs the Gadsden Purchase with Mexico.
1859	The Pig War breaks out over the border for the San Juan Islands.

Frontispiece

Page 220.

A Canoe striking on a Tree.

JOURNAL

OF THE

VOYAGES AND TRAVELS

OF

A CORPS OF DISCOVERY,

*Under the command of Capt. Lewis and Capt. Clark;
of the army of the United States,*

FROM THE MOUTH OF THE RIVER MISSOURI THROUGH
THE INTERIOR PARTS OF NORTH AMERICA
TO THE PACIFIC OCEAN,

During the Years 1804, 1805, and 1806.

CONTAINING

An authentic relation of the most interesting transactions
during the expedition; a description of the country;
and an account of its inhabitants, soil, cli-
mate, curiosities, and vegetable
and animal productions.

BY PATRICK GASS,

One of the persons employed in the expedition.

WITH GEOGRAPHICAL AND EXPLANATORY NOTES.

THIRD EDITION—WITH SIX ENGRAVINGS.

[Copy-right secured according to Law.]

PRINTED FOR MATHEW CAREY,
NO. 122 MARKET STREET,
PHILADELPHIA.

1811.

William Clark

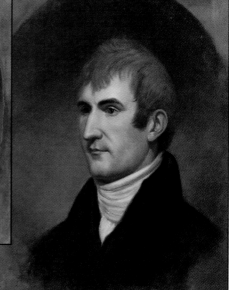

Meriwether Lewis

CHAPTER 1

Lewis and Clark's Journey

Jefferson's Dream

As a child, Thomas Jefferson heard stories about the wide Mississippi River. Might there be another river that connected the Mississippi to the Pacific Ocean? Jefferson was fascinated. And he dreamed of one day finding the answer.

Many men had tried to find what was called the Northwest Passage. President Jefferson thought that the Missouri River might be this passage. If it was, Americans could trade and sell goods on the river, perhaps all the way to the Pacific Ocean!

In 1803, Jefferson asked Congress for $2,500. He planned to use the money to organize a team of explorers. The team was known as the Corps of Discovery.

Jefferson chose his own secretary to lead the team. The man was Meriwether Lewis.

Lewis picked William Clark as his partner. The two had been friends in the army. Lewis knew they would work well together. During the cold, wet winter of 1803–1804, Lewis

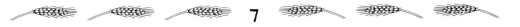

and Clark chose 28 military men. Four were army sergeants. The rest were privates. Then Lewis hired men who knew about life on the frontier. In all, there were 45 men in the group.

The two leaders kept their men busy all winter. There was much to do. They needed supplies for many months of travel. And they needed simple gifts to give to the American Indians.

Finally, it was time to set out. The group's three boats were packed with 12,000 pounds of supplies!

The First Year

The Corps of Discovery started in St. Louis. It was on the west bank of the Mississippi River. The date was May 14, 1804.

"We have chosen you carefully," Captain Lewis said. "Every man here can read and write. Each of you must keep a daily journal of our trip."

The group planned to travel up the Missouri River. They

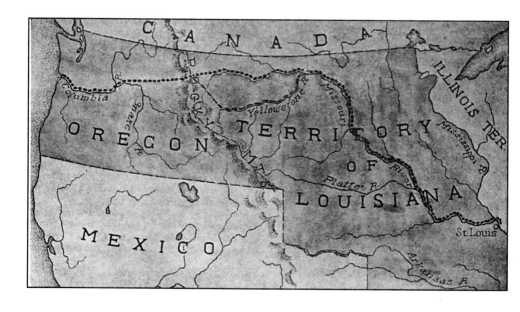

hoped to cross the Continental Divide. Then they'd sail down the Columbia River.

Hopes were high in the beginning. But moving west along the Missouri was slower than they'd expected. Soon, they fell days behind schedule.

The Corps met some friendly Sioux Indian tribes along the way. But others weren't so friendly. The Teton Sioux did not want the Americans to cross their land.

Lewis and Clark met with the Teton Sioux chief for days. They

smoked the peace pipe. They offered gifts. At last, they talked the American Indians into a peaceful crossing.

But it was late. October would soon be upon them.

At this point, the Corps of Discovery had reached the lands of the friendly Mandan Indians. This was near what is now Bismarck, North Dakota.

Winter was near. So they built a log fort. They would spend the months of snow there.

That winter, Lewis and Clark met Sacajawea. She was a Shoshone princess. She had been stolen from her tribe when she was very young.

Sacajawea promised to guide Lewis and Clark as they moved west in the spring. Her French husband, Touissant Charbonneau, would translate. He knew many American

Indian languages. A baby son would travel with them too.

Spring approached. And Lewis and Clark were eager to continue moving west. But they wanted President Jefferson to know what they had found.

Lewis chose a small group of men. "Your journals are important to the president," he said. "I want you to go back to St. Louis. From there, you are to travel to Washington, D.C. The president must know what we have found so far."

The chosen men cut down trees. They built a *barge,* or a flat boat, not much bigger than a raft. Soon they were carrying their reports to President Jefferson.

Thirty explorers stayed with Lewis and Clark. The Mandan Indians helped them prepare to go farther up the Missouri River.

More trees came down. Working with the soldiers, the American Indians helped build six strong, sleek canoes. These would be needed in the rushing spring waters of the river.

"So far," Lewis wrote in his journal, "we have had more difficulty from the Missouri than danger from the savages."

Dangerous Territory

The 30 men of the Corps of Discovery pushed west. Before long, they came to a fork in the river. Should they take the upper or lower stream? By luck, they chose the lower. It turned out to be the best way. But still it was hard travel.

The rushing waters took the explorers to a chain of five giant waterfalls. They had to hike 16 miles by land around the falls. The boats and supplies were heavy. Many trips were necessary.

The men endured several more days of hard travel and bad weather. Then they reached the spot where the Missouri met the Yellowstone River. It was an area of wild, rocky country. There were wild animals the men had never seen before. They saw mountain sheep, mules, deer, and grizzly bears.

The American Indians had warned of these wild bears. And the explorers soon believed their stories. Many times, a bear would chase a hunter at high speed even when the animal had six or seven bullets in him.

More problems with the river came each week. At times, the water flow became too strong. The men had to give up rowing. They had to walk along the shore, towing the canoes.

The group struggled through July and early August of 1805. Several times, great waterfalls stood in their way. They were forced to leave the river and hike. Up they climbed into the Rocky Mountains. As they found the top of each mountain, they saw other peaks ahead.

Would this journey never end? Lewis and Clark grew weary. The men were hungry. Sacajawea and Charbonneau were not sure how much longer the trip would take. Would no one help them here in the high country?

One day, luck was with them. They met up with a band of Shoshone. These were Sacajawea's people. And the leader of the group was her brother!

Lewis and Clark's men were given everything they needed. The Shoshone offered horses and guides from the tribe. Best of all, they had knowledge about the trails west.

Frost and snow would soon come to the high country. It was time to hurry. And it was time to leave the canoes behind. Hiding them near the river, the men loaded their supplies onto horses. Then they turned north into the Bitterroot Valley. From there, they could follow an American Indian trail west.

This trail turned out to be rocky and dangerous. Horses often fell and were hurt. Some slid down the slopes and died.

Hunting was poor. Again, the men grew hungry. They were very weak. Sometimes they were forced to shoot the dying horses. Then they'd use the meat to stay alive. Their only other food was dried bear meat and scraps of corn.

An Early Winter

On September 16, 1805, it began to snow. With only moccasins to protect their feet, the travelers were not ready for such cold. Quickly they searched for a lower, warmer trail.

Again they were lucky enough to find friendly natives. The American Indians gave the hungry men dried fish to eat. Then they pointed out where wild animals could be hunted.

Fed and partly rested, the Corps pushed west again. Within a few days, they reached the Clearwater River. This was a branch of the Snake River. This would lead them to the mighty Columbia. These waters were wide and fast. Rapids along the way would bring new dangers.

Lewis stood firm. "Winter will soon come upon us," he said. "Even here in the low country. There is no time to go by land. We must risk the high water."

Several canoes turned over and sank. But luckily, no one drowned.

They headed for the mouth of the Columbia River. They ran into more rough water—and a blinding rainstorm. The men waited on the shore for days.

They couldn't remember what dry clothes felt like. They couldn't remember what it was like to be warm.

At last, cold and pitiful, they paddled into an *estuary*. That's a place where riverwater and seawater come together. It was the Pacific Ocean! At last!

Clark stepped up to a pine tree. He carved:

"William Clark, December 3rd, 1805. By land from the U. States in 1804 and 1805."

The Corps prepared for their second winter away from home. Cutting logs from the thick forest, the men built a small winter headquarters. It was called Fort Clatsop. Then they settled down to study their journals and wait out the winter rains.

There was plenty of food there. A small river filled with fish ran just past their camp. The woods were full of animals and plants they could eat.

Meanwhile, the friendly Chinook Indians often came by. They stared at the strangers. But they caused no harm.

That winter, the explorers had sturdy log cabins. They

were thankful for enough to eat. But they were bored. And they wanted to go home. On March 23, 1806, they happily left their tiny, crowded fort. And they headed back to St. Louis.

The Return Home

Traveling through the rushing waters of the Columbia River was dangerous. Many of the group's canoes were badly damaged. Finally, they had to leave the water and pack all their goods on horses. They'd gotten the horses from the American Indians.

Throughout April, they pushed their way over the land. The friendly Nez Perce and Walla Walla tribes gave them food. And they pointed out the best mountain trails.

"We would not be alive without these red men," Lewis told Clark.

In late June, they decided to divide the Corps of Discovery into two groups. Clark led one group down the Yellowstone River. Lewis's group followed the Missouri River to the east. With joyful shouts, they reunited in August on the Missouri. And they all returned to St. Louis on September 23, 1806.

The men of the Corps of Discovery were greeted like heroes. Everyone in St. Louis turned out to cheer them.

Few people cared that Lewis and Clark had not found an all-water path to the Pacific Ocean. Instead, they had opened an endless area for Americans to settle. And it was greater than even Thomas Jefferson had thought possible.

Zebulon Pike:
In the Shadow of Glory

"Who are Lewis and Clark?" Zebulon Pike asked. "And why do they get so much glory? Doesn't anyone care what I've done for my country?"

Pike longed to be famous. His father had been a patriot in the American Revolution. Now young Pike dreamed of giving his family even more to be proud of.

When he was 15, he met General James Wilkinson. Wilkinson

was his father's commanding officer. Young Pike wanted to be like both men. So he joined the army.

Serving such a general was not wise, however. Many called Wilkinson a liar and a cheat. And they said that he was greedy.

"Be very careful," Pike's mother said. "Many say the general is not an honest man. People might not think well of you . . . if you work for him."

Some people thought Wilkinson was working for the U.S. *and* Spain. Both nations wanted land in the West.

Spain's government did not want Americans moving there. They would not be crowded out!

With Wilkinson as his guide, Pike did well in the army. Soon he was a lieutenant. But trouble lay ahead.

In 1804, General Wilkinson became governor of Upper Louisiana. This was a giant portion of the Louisiana Purchase. Now he could charge the American Indians a great deal of money for their trading licenses. Best of all, he could order the fur traders to pay him high prices.

To protect his riches, the general needed men like Pike. Such a young man could be sent to see what was going on. Wilkinson wanted news of the entire western frontier.

Pike Travels North

In August 1805, he sent Pike north up the Mississippi River. "You must find the river's source," Wilkinson ordered. "And I want to know all about the fur traders in the area."

Pike did his job well. He drew maps as he made his way north. Then he returned with his report. He was proud. He'd found the Mississippi's source. How exciting it would be to be greeted as a hero!

When he reached home, the American people were cheering. But their cheers were not for him. No one seemed to care what he had done.

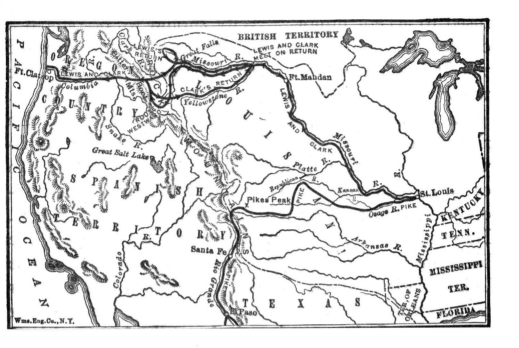

Everyone was excited about Lewis and Clark. The two men had finished the first months of their journey. Before leaving their winter camp, they had sent their journals back to President Jefferson. The stories in those journals had filled America with pride. Many now wanted to move west in the spring.

Another Mission

In 1806, Wilkinson chose Pike for a bigger job. He would travel west to the Rocky Mountains. And he would study, or *survey*, the Arkansas and Red Rivers.

"But while you are there," the general said, "find out what those Spanish are up to. Their city, Santa Fe, is a place I want to know more about."

On July 15, 1806, Pike set out with 23 men. They carefully crossed dangerous American Indian lands and pushed west.

Time passed. It was late summer. Pike knew he had been

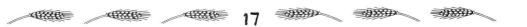

foolish. They were unprepared for the cold of fall. The men pushed on into the changing weather of the high country. By November, cold north winds pounded across the plains. The American Indians said the winter would be a hard one.

On November 15, the group spotted a huge mountain peak. Pike wrote about it in his journal. He said that it "appeared like a small blue cloud" floating over a row of far-off hills. They had heard stories of such a mountain. The American Indians had told them about it.

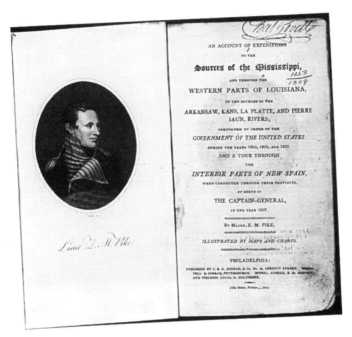

On the men pushed. After a week, Pike decided the Arkansas River's source must be quite close. He wanted to find out more about the blue mountain peak before they went on. He had his men start building a small fort next to the river.

"I will take three men with me," he said. "The rest of you can finish the fort. We will spend one day hiking to the mountain. I'm sure it is but an afternoon's walk away."

The four men traveled for two full days. They walked over hills covered with cedar trees and pitch pines. At last they thought they had reached the base of the mountain.

On November 26, Pike decided to begin the climb. The

men carried no food. They wore only light cotton overalls. They had no socks inside their thin moccasins.

"We can reach the top and return this same day," Pike said. "Don't worry about the cold."

Four days later, the men gave up. They were frozen, hungry, and sore. And they had climbed the wrong peak—a much smaller one. The "blue mountain" still stood in the distance.

Pike wrote in his journal. "It is as high again as what we climbed."

The four men dragged back to the fort. The others greeted them. Then the full party stumbled westward, lost and weak. Many were in pain from frozen hands and feet. The temperature dropped to 17 degrees below zero.

Pike and his men were forced to suffer for two more months. In January, they were found by Spanish soldiers. Arrested, they were led into Santa Fe.

Pike was asked why he had broken the law and entered Spanish lands.

He answered, "What? Is this not the Red River?"

The men were treated quite well in Santa Fe. They had

shelter and enough to eat. In April, they were told to get ready for a trip. Guided by a group of Spaniards, the men began a 63-day march back to American soil. From there, they made their way home.

False Hopes

Pike still hoped to be greeted as a hero. Lewis and Clark had just returned after their second year on the trail. And the whole nation came out to honor them. But again, Zebulon Pike was given no glory.

Word had gotten out about Wilkinson's lies and cheating. Pike's name was closely linked with the general's. Now the

people did not trust Pike.

Unlike Lewis and Clark, Pike did not receive a job from President Jefferson. He stayed in the army. But he was never appointed to the rank or duties he wanted.

War with England began again in 1812. And Pike said, "The nation will hear of my fame or my death."

In 1813, a powder keg exploded and decided his fate.

True, Pike's travels and his journals were important to the opening of the West. But he did not discover—or even climb—the famous mountain that is named for him—Colorado's Pike's Peak.

CHAPTER

Men Who Dared

Manuel Lisa was a Spaniard. A St. Louis merchant, he led 42 men up the Missouri River in 1807. They built a fort on the Yellowstone River, near where it meets the Bighorn. There they set up a fur-trapping business.

John Colter from Virginia was part of Lewis and Clark's Corps of Discovery. He later worked for the Spaniard Manuel Lisa in the fur-trapping business. In 1807, he looked for beaver and other furs. And he explored the mountains that join Wyoming, Montana, and Idaho. There he discovered the wonders of Yellowstone Park.

John Jacob Astor was a New York merchant. In 1810, he sent a group of men by ship around South America. They were to build Fort Astoria where the Columbia River meets the Pacific Ocean. At the same time, he sent 60 others west from St. Louis. They were headed for the same place. The ship blew up during an American Indian attack. The group coming by land failed to finish the trip. But they did find South Pass, an easier way to cross the Rockies.

Major Stephen H. Long and his men explored some of the same lands as Pike. Major Long dreamed of finding where the Arkansas, Platte, and Red Rivers began. While he never found the sources of those rivers, he did climb Pike's Peak. He was the first white man to do so.

Captain William Becknell left Missouri for Santa Fe in 1822. He pulled three wagons loaded with goods. He and his friends lost the trail and nearly died from desert heat. At last, they stumbled into Santa Fe. They were the first white traders to follow the American Indian Santa Fe Trail.

Jim Bridger was a mountain man and fur trapper. He was known for telling tall tales. In 1825, he sailed down the Bear River and ended up in the Great Salt Lake. The water was salty. So Bridger thought he had found a waterway to the Pacific Ocean.

Jedediah Smith was an American trader and explorer. He set out in 1826 to find trade routes to California and the Northwest. Smith wanted to find a pass across the Sierra Nevada Mountains. In 1828, he blazed a trail to Vancouver, Washington. He was killed by American Indians at age 32.

Joe Walker was known as a fine leader on the trail. In 1833, he led a party of mountain men. They crossed the Sierras from Green River, Wyoming. They found a path into California. And they were the first white men to see the Yosemite Valley. His route was later used by hundreds of wagon trains.

John Charles Fremont was a former American soldier. He explored from the Rockies to the Pacific coast. In 1842, he searched for a river spoken of by the American Indians—the Buenaventura. He hoped it would link the Pacific Ocean to the Great Salt Lake. Fremont was known as the "Pathfinder." And he wrote long, careful reports of his travels.

Kit Carson was a famous fur trapper and frontier guide. In 1842, he traveled with John C. Fremont's men to explore the Oregon Territory. In later years he was a general in the U.S. army. And he became famous fighting the Navajo Indians.

James Beckwourth was a black explorer. Both the Crow and Blackfoot made him a chief. Later, he fought for California's independence from Mexico. In 1850, he found a pass through the Sierra Nevada Mountains. It soon became an important trail for gold hunters in their rush to California.

CHAPTER

The Day the Mississippi Flowed Backward

Nobody knew it was coming.

The year was 1811. And the United States was a very young nation. The small town of New Madrid, Missouri, lay along a curve in the Mississippi River. It was two o'clock in the morning. And it was a cold December day.

The farmers of New Madrid had only a few hours left to sleep. When the sun came up, it would be time to milk the cows and feed the chickens. But for now, all was quiet. Only a few animals stamped their feet in the barns.

Suddenly, a shock like thunder passed through the earth. The ground began to move. A boom as loud as 1,000 guns filled the air.

Men, women, and children fell out of their beds. Farm animals roared in terror. The people of New Madrid felt around in the dark. They didn't understand what was happening.

They reached out, trying to hold onto moving walls. Roof boards groaned as if they were in pain. Here and there, an

older building simply fell down. All that was left was a pile of boards.

In the fields, great cracks opened in the ground. Entire houses were swallowed up.

The earth twisted. Then it closed again. The farmland rolled like waves on the ocean.

The frightened people reached for their loved ones. The shaking would stop for a moment, then begin again. The same thing would happen over and over.

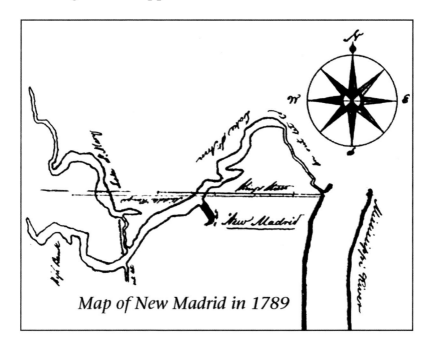

Map of New Madrid in 1789

Few families in New Madrid had lived there long. Missouri was part of the Louisiana Purchase. It had been bought from France just eight years earlier. President James Madison had asked settlers to go there to start new villages and farms. He'd hoped they would start a new frontier.

No one had said anything about earthquakes!

The farms continued to shake. But over at the nearby Mississippi River, things were much worse. The mighty river

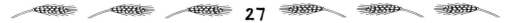

bubbled and churned. And the water turned red with mud.

Huge parts of cliffs crashed into the splashing water. They took with them whole forests of trees. In the woods along the shore, trees dipped and moved from side to side. Their top branches tangled and locked together.

Underground gases rushed into the atmosphere. A smell like rotten eggs filled the air. And people covered their noses and mouths.

The river water moved in waves, like the ocean. The Mississippi flowed over her banks, flooding everything for miles. Waves turned boats upside down or carried them miles inland.

A few brave farmers watched as the riverbed rose. It formed a six-foot waterfall. A few hours later, the rushing river erased the waterfall. And it carried it away.

Many things happened that terrible day. But one thing would never be forgotten by the people of New Madrid. The shocked farmers watched as the river bottom rose up at a place south of town. And the mighty Mississippi changed direction. The river had always flowed to the south. Now it was moving north!

There were no large towns in the area. So few people died that day. But people in four states lost their houses. The sky was black with geese and ducks. They were looking for a safe place to land.

In Washington, D.C.—1,000 miles away—buildings rocked back and forth. And windows broke.

Many brave farmers stayed to rebuild New Madrid. The ground would shake off and on for more than ten years.

America has never experienced another earthquake this strong. Nor has there ever been another one so far from where earthquakes usually happen. In fact, scientists are still trying to solve the mystery of that December day in 1811.

Everyone hopes that the Mississippi River will never again flow backward!

CHAPTER

Battle Lines

The War of 1812

Radios, telephones, fax machines, and email were not part of life in the early 1800s. If they had been, there might not have been another war between England and America.

From the end of the American Revolution, America's leaders had been bothered. The British refused to leave our country's lands along the Great Lakes. English ships ruled the Atlantic Ocean too.

They often stopped American ships. And they'd remove any British sailors who might be on board. Sometimes they "made a mistake" and took away American seamen too.

Angry members of Congress called for a fight. "Didn't we settle all this 30 years ago?" they wanted to know. "We must save America's honor. An attack against Britain's lands in Canada would show our power."

Congress warned the British to stop the boarding of American ships.

Britain said no at first. They would not stop the ship searches. The American Congressmen called for strong action. They became angrier.

On June 18, 1812, President James Madison signed a

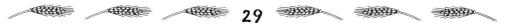

declaration of war.

But important news had not reached Congress. The British had backed down on June 16—two days earlier.

Before this news could reach Washington, D.C., American troops marched into Canada. They attacked in three places. The attacks were made in a hurry and were poorly planned. They all failed.

Americans lost the city of Detroit in August. They lost the

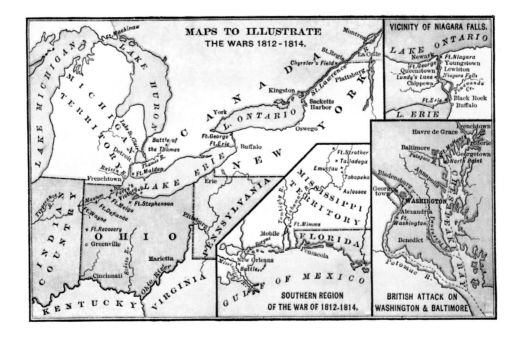

Niagara Falls territory in October. And they lost the lands along Lake Champlain in November.

American and British ships met in battle time after time. Then the British began to block entry to the American coast. Trading ships could not get through. Businesses on the Atlantic coast lost a great deal of money. Americans didn't feel safe from attack.

In 1814, the British seemed to be winning this war. Ships

and men were moving against the Americans from three directions—

- in New York along Lake Champlain
- on the Hudson River (This was an attempt to divide New England from the other states.)
- at New Orleans (This was an attempt to block the Mississippi River.)

In late summer, the British attacked Chesapeake Bay. This weakened American forces. So the British were able to march into Washington, D.C. They burned most of the government buildings.

Then they headed to the city of Baltimore. But the Americans fought bravely there at Fort McHenry. And they forced the British back. It was while watching this bitter battle that Francis Scott Key wrote the words of "The Star-spangled Banner."

Farther north, New York City was in grave danger. Ten thousand British troops moved south from Montreal, Canada. Only one thing slowed their progress—heavy losses in a battle on Lake Champlain.

Neither British nor American forces had won much ground in

Important Results of the War of 1812

- The lands around Detroit were to be part of the U.S.

- Andrew Jackson and William Henry Harrison became famous for their bravery and leadership. Jackson became our seventh President. Harrison was our ninth.

- Francis Scott Key watched a battle at Fort McHenry. Meanwhile, he wrote the words of "The Star-spangled Banner." That song later became our national anthem.

- To protect its southern coast during the war, the U.S. occupied part of Florida. Soon it was able to buy the rest of it from Spain.

the three years of fighting. Peace talks began in Ghent, Belgium. And both sides seemed eager to see the war end.

The U.S. and Great Britain signed an agreement, the Treaty of Ghent. It was signed on December 24, 1814. It called for most lands to go back to their ownership before the war.

Again, slow-moving messages changed history. Knowing nothing of the treaty, the British sailed to the Gulf of Mexico. They attacked New Orleans.

General Andrew Jackson fought a brilliant battle for the city. In January 1815, the Americans won a lopsided victory over the British forces. This was three weeks after the war had ended! In this battle, the British lost 2,000 men. And the Americans lost fewer than 100.

No one was sorry to see the war come to a close.

The Fight for the Texas Territory

Mexico gained its freedom from Spain in 1821. Then Mexico invited Americans to settle in Texas.

If a man wanted to move to this new territory, free land was waiting for him. All he had to do was become a Mexican citizen.

Many settled in Mexico. But few ever got around to becoming citizens. By 1830, 7,000 Americans lived in Texas. That's twice as many Americans as there were Mexican citizens.

Having so many Americans on his land worried General Antonio Lopez de Santa Anna. He was the president of Mexico. He would never let this huge piece of land become part of the United States!

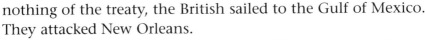
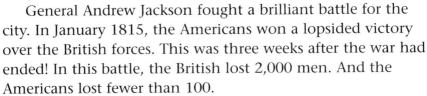

With his great army, he won an easy battle at the Alamo. Later, his men killed 371 prisoners in a town called Golidad.

Trouble along the border went on for ten years.

Treaty of Guadalupe Hidalgo

In 1844, Texan Sam Houston stopped Santa Anna's troops at the San Jacinto River. Now Americans were marching farther into Mexican territory. Before long, they had taken over Mexico City.

Santa Anna's Mexican government had never been very strong. By now, it was in a state of ruin. U.S. President James Polk found it easy to work out a treaty with the Mexicans. That 1847 agreement was the Treaty of Guadalupe Hidalgo. It gave the U.S. all the state of Texas north of the Rio Grande.

This area had long been fought over by the two nations. In addition, the U.S. received the New Mexico Territory. Arizona, New Mexico, and Utah are there today.

The Gadsden Purchase

The Treaty of Guadalupe Hidalgo had given our nation broad new lands to the west. But one more strip was needed. It lay along the southern border of Arizona, south of the Gila River. This piece of flat desert was important for a railroad route. In 1853 the U.S. sent James Gadsden to Mexico to arrange the purchase at a cost of ten million dollars. Now the U.S. border in the Southwest was complete.

Brave James Bowie

Bowie's Early Days

James Bowie had always been a bold young man. Born in Georgia in 1799, he moved west with his family. They traveled through Alabama, Mississippi, and Louisiana.

The Bowies finally settled in Texas, which was then part of Mexico.

With his brothers, Rezin and John, Jim liked to take risks. There was nothing the brothers liked better than riding alligators and chasing wild bulls.

"Guns are for sissies," young Jim Bowie bragged. "Knives are for getting close up."

When it was time to kill a bull for food, he and his brothers were ready. They would jump from their horses. Landing on top of the bull, they'd move between the long, sharp horns. Then they'd make the kill with a knife.

Hunting with knives became a problem, however. Sometimes their hands slid down the blade. A hunter's hands could be deeply cut that way.

One day, Rezin Bowie showed Jim a drawing he had made. "We need a knife with a metal guard at the top," he explained. "That will keep our hands from sliding down."

The knife Rezin drew was huge. It was 12 inches long and nearly 2 inches wide.

The brothers took the drawing to a blacksmith. The man made the knife. And stories of the Bowie knife spread through the prairie towns.

Jim Bowie was a man people noticed. He was 6' 2" with blond hair to his shoulders. He was always looking for new adventures. And he often took dangerous jobs. For these, he was paid well.

Before Bowie was 30, he had both fame and wealth. He bought a large home in the growing city of San Antonio, Texas. It was time to settle down, he'd decided.

Many Americans had settled there. But Texas was still part of Mexico. Among Bowie's neighbors was Juan Martin de Veramendi. He was one of that country's richest men.

Veramendi's daughter, Ursula, was one of the city's most beautiful young women. Bowie quickly fell in love with her. He hoped to marry her soon.

Veramendi liked the young American. But he was worried.

"If you are to marry Ursula," he said, "you must become a Mexican citizen. And you must be a Catholic."

As quickly as possible, Bowie became both.

The people of San Antonio prepared for a fine wedding.

General Antonio Lopez de Santa Anna was the bride's loving godfather. And he would be among the guests.

"Ursula is like my own daughter," said the general. "I will never forget how I held her in my arms the day she was baptized."

Santa Anna admired the bold American who would soon be part of the Veramendi family. This wedding would be a grand *fiesta!*

Two years of happiness followed. Jim and Ursula missed each other when he made long trips to buy and sell land. But Ursula knew such business was important. Their wealth grew and grew.

Then everything went wrong.

Bowie was riding back to San Antonio. He had spent three months visiting his land in Louisiana. Suddenly, he saw a friend riding out to meet him. The friend was crying.

Ursula and her parents had gone to their summer home in the hills. A terrible disease—cholera—had moved through town. It had killed hundreds of people.

Ursula's parents had died on the same day. Ursula had passed away the next afternoon.

Bowie was heartbroken. He lost interest in his land deals. For months he wandered through Louisiana and Texas. He heard more and more about Sam Houston and the Texans who wanted to be free of Mexico.

I might as well join them, he thought. I have nothing to live for now.

Bowie Joins the Fighting

General Santa Anna, once like an uncle to Jim Bowie, was now president of Mexico. He feared the Texans wanted to be part of America. This could not be allowed!

Months of trouble followed. Small battles broke out along the U.S.-Mexican border.

In the early spring of 1836, James Bowie was at the San Antonio fort, the Alamo. He was there with only 182 other men.

To defend the fort, they needed more men. And more guns. There was little food. But they would not give up. Bowie and the other Texans promised to fight to the death.

For 12 straight days, Santa Anna's 4,000 soldiers attacked the fort. The Texas defenders hardly had time to sleep or eat. They watched in fear. And the Mexicans moved closer and closer to the Alamo's walls.

They had few shells left. But the Texans returned the Mexicans' fire as best they could.

It was quiet at night. The Mexicans were sometimes surprised to hear the scratchy notes of a fiddle. The music floated through the air. Then it was followed by the sad tones of a bagpipe.

The fiddler was the frontier scout Davy Crockett. The man on bagpipes was John McGregor. He was a lad from Scotland. And he'd settled in Texas and joined the fight for freedom.

Jim Bowie did not lead the Alamo's fight for long. He had caught a bad cold. And a fall from a ladder had made him very weak.

On the second day of battle, burning with fever, he crawled onto his cot. Bowie was too sick to fight.

On the afternoon of March 5, 1836, the Alamo's cannons were silent. The supply of cannonballs was low. So they had to be saved.

The American defenders waited for the final battle.

The Final Battle at the Alamo

As the sun came up on March 6, a line of Mexican soldiers charged the Alamo. They carried ladders. As they reached the top of the walls, the Texans shot them down with rifle fire.

Crockett and his men stood ready. They were on the south side of the courtyard. They stopped another line of Mexicans climbing the walls. Still more Mexican soldiers ran forward.

Two of the Mexican leaders tried a new idea. They led their men away from the south wall. And they marched to the western side. The Mexicans on the east went around to the north.

These changes made the Alamo's cannons useless. Now they were facing the wrong way!

The Texans had no choice but to climb on top of the walls to shoot. Now they were easy to see. One by one, they were shot down.

Bowie lay on a cot in the Alamo's chapel. He was too sick to raise his head.

Crockett had come to him the night before. "Here are two loaded pistols," Crockett had said. "And beside you is your Bowie knife."

James Bowie would not die alone. A great many Mexican soldiers would die with him. That was his promise.

When the fighting was over, dead men lay everywhere. There were 680 bodies. Only 183 of them were Texans. Among them were Davy Crockett and James Bowie.

The Mexican dictator Santa Anna looked down upon the bodies. He saw Bowie, the young husband of his godchild. They had once been like family.

"He was too much a man to be treated like a dog," said Santa Anna. "See that he is given a decent burial. For James Bowie was a brave man."

CHAPTER 6

Measuring the Prairie

Settlers continued to move west. They needed ways to measure their new land.

They learned one method from the Spanish. Two men on horses were needed for the job. One man held a long piece of cord. This cord was 100 *varas*. A *vara* is about 33 inches long.

One rider held the cord and kept his horse very still. The second man took the other end of the cord. Then he rode past the first man.

When the cord was pulled straight, the second man stopped. Then he held his horse still. And the first man rode by.

They took turns until they came to the end of the property. Then they counted the number of rope lengths. And they multiplied that number by 100. This is how they figured the length or width of the property.

Another early method of measurement used a wagon's wheel. The settlers figured the distance around the wheel, or the wheel's *circumference*. Then they tied a bit of cloth around one of the wheel's spokes.

As the wheel rolled forward, they counted the number of times the cloth knot went around. They multiplied that by the circumference. And this is how they measured the distance the wheel had rolled.

    39

Letters from the Frontier

In the 1840s, many eastern families headed west. They rode in heavy wagons. And they traveled through dangerous country. All this was to build homes in unknown lands.

The three main paths west were the Oregon Trail, Mormon Trail, and the Sante Fe Trail.

On the following pages are some letters. They might have been written by the son and daughter of such a family.

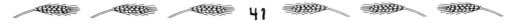

Wyoming Territory
September 9, 1847

Dear Grandpa,

Pa has asked me to write to you. He says you must wonder how we are.

Things have been pretty good since we left your house in Missouri. How is everybody in Independence?

Do you remember how big you thought our wagon was? After you said that, Pa started to load it up. He put in a plow and a pile of spare wagon parts. Ma's barrel of best dishes. And two shovels and some smaller tools. Then he packed all the food he could. There was hardly any room left for Ma and Deborah and me. Pa rides up front. So do the guns and ammunition.

We needed a safe place for the seed. We looked for a spot where rain wouldn't come in. Pa says—

"What good is seed if it gets wet and sprouts before we find a place to plant it?"

There were 53 families in our wagon train. Sometimes I thought we'd never get going in the morning. It seemed that somebody's horse or ox would always wander off. Just when it was time to set out after breakfast!

Deborah and I learned a very important lesson. And that was to not chase our chickens back into their crate before all the wagons were hitched up.

Some people tried bringing cows on the trail. It was sad. They all died from eating nothing but prairie grass. Now Pa says a cow's the first thing we'll buy after we have our house started. If we can find a cow, that is. I really miss drinking milk!

Well, Grandpa, it's time for me to go. Pa is out cutting down cottonwood trees for our house. I need to help him drag them back here to the clearing.

Your grandson,
Johnny

Wyoming Territory
March 6, 1848

Dear Grandpa,

I know Pa has written to you. But I wanted to send a letter too. We all miss you. Last night, we ate the last pieces of maple sugar candy you sent with us. I remember how you used to buy it for me at the store in Independence.

Ma and Pa have decided to stay in Wyoming. So we won't be starting west again this spring.

Pa finished making all our furniture during the winter. As soon as it is warm enough, he will cut out windows so we have some light. The windows will be oiled paper at first. But Ma says someday we will have glass!

Deborah and I will soon move our bedrolls up to the loft. It's above the fireplace. It's a cozy place to sleep! Too bad I can't have it all to myself.

Now for the best news of all. As soon as the snow melts, Pa will build a room for you. He even showed me a plan he drew.

Pa knows a family headed this way in the spring. Before we left Independence, they promised to bring you along. Ma will write and tell you what to bring.

Johnny

Wyoming Territory
October 14, 1847

Dear Emily,

We did it! We made it to Wyoming! Sometimes I didn't believe it would really happen. It's been so many weeks since I said good-bye to you in Independence.

The trail was bumpy. Sometimes I thought the day would never end. Do you remember how afraid I was of the American Indians? Well, none of them ever hurt us. But sometimes a horse went after grass too far from the wagons. And sometimes we never saw that horse again.

Pa is teaching Johnny to use the rifle. In Independence, he said no guns until a boy was 14. Johnny's only just turned 12. But out here on the prairie, boys learn to shoot sooner.

I guess that's good. Because we can't eat unless Pa and Johnny shoot something. They usually shoot a deer, some rabbits, or a prairie chicken or two. Pa says he'll try to get us a wild turkey soon.

Pa says he'll teach me to shoot too. He says a girl of 15 has to know how to protect her home. Just in case of trouble.

Pa and Johnny cut down cottonwood trees to build our house. I'm glad we got here when we did. If it had been any later, they would have had to build just a shack, or a *lean-to*. Those are never warm enough. And you have to keep a bonfire going at the open end all the time.

Our log house has one room and a dirt floor. But Ma says there isn't time to build anything more. Because the snows will come soon.

Ma and I gathered sticks, mud, and moss. We used those things to close up the holes between the logs. That helps keep the wind out.

Now Pa is finishing a mud fireplace. He says he'll build a better one. As soon as we can find enough rocks.

You should have seen us building fires on the wagon trail. It was awful! You remember the huge prairie animals called buffalo? Well, we didn't see many of them. But we knew they had been around.

(Can you figure out what I mean, Emily? Think about it. The buffalo eats. Then something drops on the ground and dries. Now do you understand?)

Well, what the buffalo drops is as big as a dinner plate! They're called *buffalo chips*. And they burn into a good, hot fire. The smaller boys and girls had the job of picking them up. I even had to help a few times. Ugh!

Please try to write to me, dear Emily. I miss you so. There were other girls on the wagon train. But their families went on west. We stopped to build. So there are no families nearby.

Send a letter to Fort Laramie. I'm sure it will get to me that way.

Your lonely friend,
Deborah

Wyoming Territory
May 2, 1848

Dear Emily,

Oh, at last, dear friend! Your letter came yesterday. A scout from Fort Laramie was headed this way. He came right to our door.

I was so hungry for news of my school friends in Independence. Ma teaches us at home. But there is talk of bringing a teacher to our settlement. We have more families around us now. So we really need a school.

Our house is looking better. Pa put in a wood floor. And he pounded pegs into the wall for our extra clothes. Ma has a peg for her Sunday dress. And I have one for mine.

There's a table and four benches. A big bed for Ma and Pa. And a loft where Johnny and I sleep. Ma hung an old quilt down the middle. So it's almost like having our own rooms.

For a while, we wore shoes made of animal skins. It doesn't sound very pretty, I know. But Pa turns the skins so the animal fur is inside. Our feet stay nice and warm that way. I think you would like them.

Two men are building a general store. It will be ten miles away. Pa is saving animal skins to trade. And Ma will make butter and cheese to swap for tea and chocolate.

Johnny is brave about going into beehives. Pa says he can keep anything he trades for his honey.

So you see, dear Emily, life will be easier on the prairie this summer. The snow is melting. And we hope for fine crops. I miss Independence. But I'm not sure I could leave this new land. If you saw the beautiful sky here, you would understand.

Please write again!

Your friend,
Deborah

CHAPTER 8

Peralta's Gold

Spanish priests had come to California long before American settlers moved west. The priests built missions. And they began to teach the American Indians.

When Mexico won independence from Spain, California flew the Mexican flag. In 1848, the United States took California from Mexico. That was during the Mexican-American War.

Just before peace came to the land, something big happened. Gold was discovered on the American River in northern California.

Settlers poured into the territory from all parts of the world. Between 1848 and 1860, California's population grew from 26,000 to 380,000! At last, the United States was settled from the Atlantic to the Pacific coasts.

Just two borders remained unsure. One was between Arizona and Mexico. The other was between Canada and the state of Washington.

The following story shows just how the borders affected people. It's a powerful story of gold, daring men, and puzzling events.

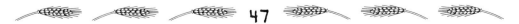

A Father's Quest

The story begins in 1847 on Don Miguel Peralta's cattle ranch. Peralta was a citizen of Sonora, Mexico. His property served as a home for 500 men, women, and children. Indeed, it was as large as many towns.

Peralta was wild with anger! His daughter, Rosita, had fallen in love with Carlos, a handsome ranch hand.

"This is not the right man for my lovely Rosita!" Peralta stormed. "I must get rid of him."

The young man feared Peralta's anger. So he ran away, traveling north. He escaped into the rocky, unknown lands near the Gila River.

Peralta paced around his ranch. Carlos had not promised to stay away. Peralta called Wolf's Nose. He was a fine tracker from the nearby American Indian village.

"Go after him," Peralta ordered. "Be sure he goes far north and never comes back."

Wolf's Nose asked for only one ranch hand to go with him. Peralta agreed.

Gold!

Six weeks passed. There was no news. Finally, lookouts spotted something. A man was limping across the prairie

toward the ranch. It was Wolf's Nose.

"We found Carlos," he said. "The boy showed us a fortune in gold. He said it was from a faraway mountain. Far into the desert."

This news delighted Peralta. These riches were right there in northern Sonora!

Wolf's Nose explained what had happened.

Carlos and the two trackers had loaded their bags with gold. Soon they were on their way back south to the Peralta ranch.

But danger lay ahead. A week into their travels, they came to a deep, rushing stream. The men were not sure how deep it was. They were carrying many pounds of gold.

Quickly, the three were swept into the roaring waters. Only Wolf's Nose came out alive.

Wolf's Nose's report of gold sent excitement through the ranch. Peralta immediately gathered 50 men and sent them north to find more riches. In three weeks, they were back. And their saddlebags were stuffed with gold. Here was a fortune for the taking.

Peralta knew he couldn't run a huge ranch and mine gold too. So he began to change his life's work. He sold his cattle and his tools. Everything he did was orderly and careful. There seemed no need to hurry.

Fate, however, would take him on another path.

News reached Sonora about the Treaty of Guadalupe Hidalgo. All fighting in the Mexican-American War was ended. The border between the two nations would forever lie south of the Gila River. The state of Sonora, Mexico, would no longer reach so far north.

Peralta was shocked! His secret mine would soon be on the other side of the border!

Upset by the terrible news, he made one last try to rescue his fortune. If he waited, he wouldn't be able to remove the gold from the new lands called Arizona.

"The gold is no longer in my country," he groaned.

He quickly made a plan. He didn't want the American government to guess what he was up to.

He formed a group of 400 men and 1,000 animals. It would be a huge pack train. The greatest example of treasure-hunting the West had ever seen.

He and his men went back over the path to what is now called the Superstition Mountains. And they found the mine. They loaded the animals with a huge fortune in gold. Then they started south again. How the people of Sonora would cheer for them!

Excited by their success, the men rode along happily. They dreamed of a lifetime of riches.

Peralta's Tragic End

At this point, Peralta and his men may have been careless. The desert lay on all sides. It seemed peaceful and secure.

The pack train started out of the valley of the Superstition Mountains. Just then, there was an outcry. And a war party of Apache Indians rushed toward them. The attack was bitter. And Peralta and the other Sonorans were wiped out in 30 minutes.

Of the 400 men, only two young boys lived. They crept south by day. And they slept in bushes at night. A month later, they reached the ranch. And they shared the terrible news.

Still Searching

In later years, the two young men tried many times to find the mine. They were unsuccessful.

Around 1875, it is believed that one of these men told the tale of hidden gold to Jacob Waltz. He was an old German miner.

Soon after that, the bodies of two young men were found on the mountain. They had been shot many times. Their

deaths remained a mystery. No one was ever arrested.

People in the nearby desert called Jacob Waltz "Old Snow Beard, the Dutchman." He claimed to have found Peralta's gold mine. But most historians don't believe it. The rocks around his diggings were nothing like those that hold gold.

In 1891, Waltz died. The secret of the gold died with him.

Hundreds of men and women have searched for the Lost Dutchman Mine. They still do so today. Some have searched and lived to tell about it. Some have never been seen again.

What might have happened if there had been no boundary change? Would Peralta have claimed his gold and lived?

That's something we'll never know.

CHAPTER 9

The Pig War

A battle seemed ready to explode in the Pacific Northwest for more than 12 years. It would send the United States into a war with Great Britain.

What was the reason for this military time bomb? The death of a pig.

It all began with an 1846 treaty. It was between the U.S. and Great Britain. Some of the words were unclear. The U.S. was to have full ownership of the Oregon Territory. That was a huge piece of land. It includes what is now Washington, Oregon, Idaho, and parts of Montana and Wyoming.

The problem was the line between the U.S. and Britain's Canadian lands. Part of the border was to lie in the middle of a channel. But there were really two channels.

If you followed one of these, the small island of San Juan was American. If you followed the other channel, it was British territory. Because the agreement was so hard to understand, both the U.S. and Great Britain considered San Juan Island theirs. And settlers from both countries wanted to live there.

Britain's Hudson's Bay Company started a salmon fishery on San Juan in 1850. They started a sheep ranch three years later.

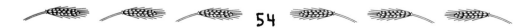

At the same time, the United States declared the island to be part of the state of Washington. Soon, about two dozen Americans had settled there. The Americans and the British did not always get along well.

The Pig Started It All

Trouble came on June 15, 1859. A huge black pig broke through a fence. The animal belonged to Britain's Hudson's Bay Company in Canada.

The pig entered the farm of an American settler, Lyman Cutler. Cutler had a short temper. He looked out his window that sunny morning. And he saw the hungry pig digging in his potato patch.

Angry, Cutler ran from his log cabin. He was carrying his rifle. Taking careful aim, he shot and killed the animal.

Immediately, the British warned that they would arrest Cutler. He had killed the property of their powerful Hudson's Bay Company.

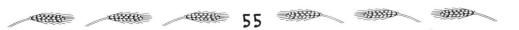

Shocked, the American settlers on San Juan Island asked the U.S. army to protect them. In reply, the U.S. sent 66 soldiers to the island.

News of this reached Governor James Douglas. He was from the British Crown Colony.

"What are American soldiers doing on San Juan Island?" he demanded. He quickly sent three British warships toward the island.

Douglas had firm orders, however. The American soldiers were to be driven off the island. But there was to be no shooting. Douglas was warned that he must not involve two great nations in a war. Not over a pig, anyway!

Another 64 American men arrived. They would not be scared off. They gathered at the south end of the island.

Nearby was Lyman Cutler's farm, where it had all started.

By August 31, 461 men were crowded into American Camp. With them were 14 cannons. Just off the island sailed five British warships. They carried 167 guns and 2,000 men.

The President Gets Involved

In Washington, President James Buchanan was alarmed.

"How has the action of one young farmer grown into near war?" he wondered.

Buchanan sent General Winfield Scott, commanding general of the U.S. Army, to San Juan Island. The president said, "It would be shocking if two great nations went to war over one small island."

Letters passed between Scott and the British governor. At last, the two men agreed. A force of 100 men from each nation would occupy San Juan Island. They would stay until a final agreement could be reached.

In March 1860, 100 British Royal Marines landed at the island's north end. Sixteen miles away were the 100 soldiers at

President James Buchanan

American Camp. An uneasy peace was in place.

Twelve years passed. The United States was busy with the Civil War. The question of who owned a small island did not seem important.

The Kaiser Decides

San Juan Island remained under two flags. Then Britain and the U.S. signed the Treaty of Washington in 1871.

At that time, the matter was turned over to Kaiser Wilhelm I of Germany. The British and Americans trusted the German leader to decide for them.

On October 21, 1872, the Kaiser ruled in favor of the United States. The British forces packed up and left San Juan Island. This made it the last place in our country to be occupied by the British.

Peace had come at last. America's borders were decided for all time. And the only loss of life in the long, final struggle was a single pig.

CHAPTER 10

The St. Louis Arch:
A Monument to the Dream

A tall, gleaming arch stands on the west bank of the Mississippi River. It reaches 630 feet into the air. And it is the tallest monument in the United States. It honors the brave men and women who traveled west to settle new lands.

For many years, America stretched only from the Atlantic Ocean to the Mississippi River. In 1803, however, our country bought a huge piece of land from France.

This was the Louisiana Purchase. And it tripled America's size.

America grew and prospered for more than 100 years. Still, there was no monument to America's pioneers.

In 1936, President Franklin D. Roosevelt signed some papers. These papers created the Jefferson National Expansion Memorial. It was to be built in Missouri.

Along the riverfront in St. Louis, 40 blocks were cleared. But no one had decided what the monument would look like.

Then World War II got in the way. Nothing could be done until peace came to the world.

That happened in 1945. Now the citizens of St. Louis were in a hurry. They wanted the memorial to rise on their side of the Mississippi River. The land was ready.

What should the monument look like? How big should it be? A committee was formed to decide such things. Right away, the committee called for a contest. They hoped for many good ideas.

The best idea came from Eero Saarinen, an architect from Finland. His tall steel arch would look like a doorway. It would honor the pioneers who had bravely moved west.

People saw Saarinen's drawings. And they began to call the monument "our St. Louis Arch."

The arch Saarinen drew was based on a hanging chain. Imagine that you hung a chain between two buildings. Then you turned that loop upside down. You would be left with the shape of the St. Louis Arch.

Years of planning followed. At last, all was ready. The first pieces went into place on February 12, 1963. The difficult job of building such a monument would take two and a half years.

There were many dangers. Huge steel pieces had to be lifted into the air. The workers hung by belts high above the city streets. Each week, the monument rose. Finally, it was 630 feet tall. That was taller than any other building in St. Louis. By good luck, not one worker fell.

Photo courtesy of St. Louis Post Dispatch

Today, you can visit this memorial. Between the two legs,
you will find an underground museum. A movie, *Monument*

to the Dream, shows how the arch was built. And there are displays about the early pioneer days.

You can even ride to the top. Small, round elevators each hold six people. They travel inside the legs of the arch. In four minutes, your elevator will have risen 630 feet.

At the top is a long, narrow room with many windows. You can look eastward across the Mississippi River. You can see into Illinois. Many pioneers came from that direction.

Or you can turn around and look westward. Maybe you can pretend that you were a pioneer.

And their dream will be yours too.

Index